GREAT BOOK OF
Zany Jokes

• • • • •

Matt Rissinger
& Philip Yates

Illustrated by Lucy Corvino

 Sterling Publishing Co., Inc. New York

To Mom and Dad with love—P.Y.
To Maggie, Rebecca and Emily with thanks—M.R.

Library of Congress Cataloging-in-Publication Data

Rissinger, Matt.
    Great book of zany jokes / Matt Rissinger & Philip Yates ;
illustrated by Lucy Corvino.
        p.   cm.
    Includes index.
    ISBN 0-8069-0470-4
    1. Wit and humor, Juvenile. [1. Jokes.] I. Yates, Philip,
1956– . II. Corvino, Lucy, ill. III. Title.
PN6163.R53   1994
818'.5402—dc20   93-39189
                                                    CIP
                                                     AC

10 9 8 7 6 5 4 3 2 1

First paperback edition published in 1995 by
Sterling Publishing Company, Inc.
387 Park Avenue South, New York, N.Y. 10016
© 1994 by Matt Rissinger & Philip Yates
Illustrations © 1994 by Lucy Corvino
Distributed in Canada by Sterling Publishing
℅ Canadian Manda Group, One Atlantic Avenue, Suite 105
Toronto, Ontario, Canada M6K 3E7
Distributed in Great Britain and Europe by Cassell PLC
Villiers House, 41/47 Strand, London WC2N 5JE, England
Distributed in Australia by Capricorn Link (Australia) Pty Ltd.
P.O. Box 6651, Baulkham Hills, Business Centre, NSW 2153, Australia
Manufactured in the United States of America
All rights reserved

Sterling ISBN 0-8069-0470-4 Trade
            0-8069-0471-2 Paper

CONTENTS

1. SOUP TO NUTS

SAL: I hate alphabet soup.
CAL: What's wrong with it?
SAL: Do I have to spell it out for you?

CUSTOMER: How did this fly get in my soup?
WAITER: Must have parachuted in.

Knock-knock!
  Who's there?
Soup du jour.
  Soup du jour who?
Soup du jour
(shut the door),
it's cold outside!

Knock-knock!
  Who's there?
Broth
  Broth who?
Broth-er, this is good soup.

What's a scarecrow's favorite fruit?
Straw-berries.

How do you make an orange turn over?
Tickle its navel.

What happened when the grape saw into the future?
It started raisin a fuss.

What would you get if you crossed tropical fruit with a cartoon hero?
Papaya the Sailor Man.

What's a raisin's favorite amusement park?
Grape Adventure.

What did the cannibal wife give her husband when he came home late?
The cold shoulder.

What do cannibals call a shipwreck?
Lunch.

Why did the little girl give her allowance to the bread makers?
She wanted to help the kneady.

Where do pastry chefs warm up?
In the batter box.

How do you strain vegetables?
Give them lots of homework.

Why was the vegetarian arrested?
He was caught with hot potatoes.

How do corn kernels propose marriage?
They pop the question.

Where do vegetables go to get married?
To a Justice of the Peas.

How do vegetables serve their country?
They join the Peas Corps.

What did the frog drink when he went on a diet?
Diet Croak.

What do you call a mannequin on a weight-loss program?
A crash diet dummy.

What do you get when you cross an exercise video with melted cheese?
Jane Fondue Workout Tape.

What do you call in case of a hunger emergency?
Dine 11 (911).

JOE: I'm so hungry I could eat a horse.
MOE: I find that hard to swallow.

What kind of veggies do they eat at the North Pole?
  Snow peas.

What kind of vegetables are sailors afraid of?
  Leeks (leaks).

What happens when lettuce is arrested for a crime?
  It's innocent until proven wilty.

What do mannequins put on their salads?
  Window dressing.

What's green and crunchy and makes a low noise?
  Pickle-o (piccolo).

What would you get if you crossed a gas with raisins and nuts?
  Vapor Trail Mix.

Knock-knock!
  Who's there?
Pecan.
  Pecan who?
Pecan the cookie jar and see if there's any left.

How does the world's smallest person say goodbye?
  With a microwave.

2. DOWN TO EARTH

What dinosaur is at home on the range?
Tyrannosaurus Tex.

What dinosaur likes to eat enchiladas?
Tyrannosaurus Mex.

TEACHER: Where is the Red Sea?
HOWARD: On the third line of my report card.

CRUISE TRAVELLER: How close are we to land?
CRUISE CAPTAIN: About three miles.
CRUISE TRAVELLER: In which direction?
CRUISE CAPTAIN: Straight down.

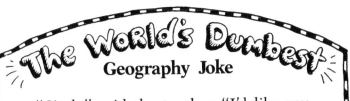

The World's Dumbest
Geography Joke

"Cindy," said the teacher, "I'd like you to come up to the map and point out Cuba." Mary went to the front of the room and pointed to Cuba on the map.

"Very good," said the teacher. "Now tell me who discovered Cuba."

"I did," said Mary.

TRAVELLER: Is this my plane?

STEWARD: No, it belongs to the airport.

TRAVELLER: Very funny. Can I take it to Paris?

STEWARD: Okay, but bring it back first thing in the morning.

TEACHER: What foreign country sends us sugar?

BILLY: We don't get sugar from foreign countries. We borrow it from next door.

Where do snakes go on vacation?
Venom-Zuela.

What is the best game to play on misty days?
Leapfog.

What do you always find at the end of a tunnel?
The letter "l."

the woRLd's WeiRdest
Weather Joke

When Julius Caesar saw a storm coming, he consulted his weather wizard.

"What's it going to be like?" he asked the wizard.

"Hail, Caesar!" replied the wizard.

How do you wrap a gift for a weatherman?
With a rain-bow.

Why does winter always seem like the longest season?
Because it comes in one year and out the other.

How do Eskimos like to travel to Alaska?
On icicles built for two.

The World's Silliest

Alaska Fable

Two Eskimos went fishing in their kayak. After a while it got so cold they lit a fire in the boat. The boat soon went up in flames and sunk.

MORAL: You can't have your kayak and heat it, too.

What would you get if you crossed a rock formation with a bison?

A bluff-alo.

What mountain range sings religious songs?

The Hymn-alayas.

What do you call four stone presidents with a skin condition?

Mount Rashmore (Rushmore).

Where do astronauts go for refreshments when they're on the Red Planet?

Mars bars.

A chameleon walked into a travel office.

"Where would you like to go?" asked the travel agent.

"No place in particular," said the chameleon. "I'm just looking for a change."

3. ORDER IN THE SPORT!

When did the bratty gymnast win the competition?
When she finally got off her high horse.

LARRY: Can you spot me on the parallel bars?
BARRY: Sure, you're right there.

What kind of dancing do crash dummies enjoy?
Brake dancing.

What's blue and cuddly, and you can play baseball on it?
Astro-Smurf.

CANNIBAL FATHER: Well, how did your team do today?

CANNIBAL SON: We creamed them.

CANNIBAL FATHER: In the finals?

CANNIBAL SON: No, in the main course.

CANNIBAL SON: Can I eat the batter, mom?

CANNIBAL MOM: Yes, but only if he strikes out.

What happened to the baseball player who was late for dinner?

His wife threw him out at home.

What do you call the player behind home plate on an all St. Bernard baseball team?

The dog catcher.

What's the difference between a good sportsman and an umpire?

One plays by the rules, the other rules on the plays.

How did the mermaid convince the ballplayer to join her in the ocean?

She told him there were 20,000 leagues under the sea.

What vegetable has the highest batting average?

Veggie Jackson.

SANDY: Who lives in a church bell tower and plays football?

RANDY: The halfback of Notre Dame.

What did the football coach say when the giant dropped the ball?

"Fe-fi-fo-fumble!"

What did the football coach say when he learned his piggy bank was stolen?

"I want my quarter back!"

What do you get when you cross a boxer with orange juice?

Fruit punch.

What do you hear when you cross a fighter with a telephone?

A boxing ring.

Why do boxing announcers make good storytellers?

They give blow-by-blow accounts.

Who wears a hat with bells and makes John McEnroe laugh?

Tennis Court Jester.

What's round, flat and makes a terrible racket?

Tennis the Menace.

VINNY: My dad invented a mint for long distance runners.

WINNY: What does he call it?

VINNY: An out-of-breath mint.

WILLY: What do you get when you cross track shoes with comedy?

BILLY: A running joke.

MOE: What would you get if you crossed running shoes with matches?

JOE: Reeboks that burn up the road.

What ancient Egyptian beauty queen wore spiked running shoes?

Cleats-o-patra.

How were Adam and Eve kept from gambling?
Their pair of dice (paradise) was taken from them.

Where do hockey players stay in New York?
Empire Skate Building.

What does a dentist on a hockey team specialize in?
Puck teeth.

What would you get if you crossed a race car
with a bellboy?
Vrooom service.

Why did the zombie lose the race?
He was dead last.

What kind of clothes do parachutists wear?
  Jump suits.

PARATROOPER LEADER: What's the most important
    rule to remember when jumping?
PARATROOPER STUDENT: Chute first, ask questions
    later.

What would you get if you crossed a ghost with a
soccer ball?
  Field ghouls.

What felines have the most strikes against them?
  Bowling alley cats.

What would you get if you crossed an athlete
with a pumpkin?
  Jock-o'-lantern.

What country did the python represent at the
Olympics?
  The United Snakes of America.

Can kids learn to fly jet planes?
  Of course, but they have to use training wheels.

What did the swimming pool say to the
springboard?
  "You're diving me crazy!"

Two inexperienced hunters went hunting in the woods. Before long they got lost.

"Don't worry," said the first hunter. "I heard that when you're lost you should fire three shots in the air so somebody will hear you."

They fired three shots in the air and waited. A half hour later they tried it again and still no one came. Finally they decided to try it a third time.

"This better work," said the second hunter nervously. "These're our last arrows."

What can you do on a bicycle that you can't do on a unicycle?
Ring the bell.

How do nine golfers press their shirts?
With nine irons.

What did the golfing caterpillar grow up to be?
A putter-fly.

What do doughnuts and good golfers have in common?
A hole in one.

What do championship golfers and playgrounds have in common?
A good swing.

What do crocodiles drink before a big race?
Ali-Gatorade.

How do you make a California shake?
Hold the glass still and shake the street.

What's a frog's favorite sport?
Fly fishing.

How do rabbits stay in shape?
They do hare-robics.

What do athletic geniuses wear?
Think-tank tops.

What has blonde hair, lifts weights, and buzzes?
Bar-bee.

the WORLD's Weirdest
Sheep Story

Phil and Will built a skating rink in the middle of a pasture. One day a shepherd leading his flock decided to take a shortcut across the rink. The sheep, however, were afraid of the ice and wouldn't cross it. Desperate, the shepherd began tugging them to the other side.

"Look at that," remarked Phil to Will. "That guy is trying to pull the wool over our ice!"

What pet did the race car driver buy?
A lap dog.

What kind of hats do crash dummies wear?
Demolition derbies.

How do automobiles protect themselves?
With kar-ate.

4. CHUCKLE UP FOR SAFETY...

What's the first thing clowns do when they get in a car?
Chuckle-up.

What's the first thing boxers do when they get in a car?
Knuckle-up.

What's the first thing you should do if your car gets stuck in the ocean?
Call for an undertow truck.

Why was the cautious lifeguard fired?
He kept people wading too long.

TEACHER: Why are you late?

DENNIS: My little brother fell through the ice and I rescued him.

TEACHER: Is he all right?

DENNIS: Yes, but he's not allowed to play in the freezer anymore.

Why do chickens stay out of the sun?
  To avoid getting fried.

What kind of suntan lotion do rabbits wear?
  Hoppertone.

Why did the father put his son under a beach umbrella?
  To avoid son burn.

Why did Smokey the Bear retire?
He was burned out.

SAFETY INSTRUCTOR: What should you do if your
    smoke alarm goes off?
CLASS JOKER: Run after it.

What do rock stars do if they catch fire?
Stop, rock and roll.

What do janitors do if they catch fire?
Stop, mop and glo.

What do boxers do if they catch fire?
Stop, drop and roll with the punches.

What kind of clothing would you find at a fire
sale?
Blazers.

What kind of underwear is useful at a fire?
Panty hose.

Safety Sign in Karate
Cooking Class

WOK, DO NOT RUN

What would you get if you crossed a dentist with a weasel?

The Tooth Ferret.

How do hard rockers keep their teeth straight?

Heavy metal braces.

SAFETY TEACHER: How do we prevent mushroom poisoning?

CLASS JOKER: Lock the medicine cabinet so mushrooms can't get in.

FIRST AID TEACHER: How do you call an ambulance?

CLASS JOKER: "Hey, ambulance!"

How do geniuses clean their ears?
With I.Q. Tips.

WILL: My sister swallowed a watch.
BILL: Does it hurt?
WILL: Only when she tries to wind it.

What type of pill needs an alarm clock?
A sleeping pill.

What happened to the worker who fell into the vat of bubble gum?
He got chewed out.

Knock-knock!
Who's there?
Hygiene.
Hygiene who?
Hygiene, how ya' doin'?

What's the most dangerous flight at the airport?
A flight of stairs.

What were the crash dummy's last words?
"Give me a brake."

5. TAKE MY ANIMAL— PLEASE!

What's brown, has eight legs and a big trunk?
A spider coming back from vacation.

What's black and white, furry, and doesn't ever want to grow up?
Peter Pan-da.

What would you get if you crossed a minnow with a monkey?
A shrimpanzee.

28

What's a cat's favorite vegetable?
  Birds' Eye.

How does your cat feel when it gets stuck inside a medicine bottle?
  Cat-a-tonic.

What do cats put on after a bath?
  Purr-fume.

What do cats use to keep their breath fresh?
  Mouse wash.

The World's Dumbest Cat Joke

A man walked into a laundry run by cats.

"Excuse me," said the man to the cat in charge, "but can you get this milk stain out?"

"Don't worry," said the cat, "we'll have it licked in a minute."

What would you get if you crossed a dog with lunch meat?
  A cocker spamiel.

What dog keeps stepping on your toes?
  A Mexican careless (hairless).

What dogs work for the telephone company?
Labrador receivers.

What do you call a Labrador retriever that eats only plants?
A fetch-etarian.

What did one dog detective say to the other dog detective?
"I think someone is tailing us."

Why did the puppy go to the hair salon?
To get a shampoodle.

TEDDIE: My dog is a carpenter.
EDDIE: What makes you say that?
TEDDIE: Last night he made a bolt for the door.

What did the dog say to the flea?
"I'll be your host this evening."

Why do salmons like mornings the best?
It's the spawn (dawn) of a new day.

Why was the comic fish fired?
His act smelt.

Who visits good little mermaids each spring to deliver eggs and candy?
The Oyster Bunny.

What do big white whales play cards with?
  Moby Deck.

Who is the saddest whale?
  Mopey Dick.

Who's the world's greatest whale magician?
  Moby Trick.

What's big, blows water from its spout, and turns up once every 76 years?
  Whaley's Comet.

Where do shellfish gamble?
  At the Clams Casino.

Where do mother octopuses shop for clothes for their children?
  Squids R Us.

What is the favorite fish of the Three Musketeers?
Swordfish.

CUSTOMER: May I have a pair of alligator shoes?
SALESMAN: Certainly. What size is your alligator?

How do you get rid of an alligator?
Call a fumi-gator.

What pig writes to another pig?
A pen pal.

What did one sleepy pig say to the other sleepy pig?
"Stop hogging the blankets!"

What do bumblebees wear to the beach?
Bee-kinis.

What do bees brush their hair with?
Honeycombs.

Where do hornets go when they're sick?
The waspital.

What kind of bug keeps Santa Claus company?
Chimney (Jiminy) Cricket.

Who is the world's greatest story-telling bug?
Ants (Hans) Christian Andersen.

What books do fireflies like?
Matchbooks.

The World's Silliest Insect Songs

"I'm in the Mood for Larva (Love)" by
Kate R. Pillar

"Leggy Sue" by Cent I. Pede

"Jump" by Gus Hopper

"You Bite (Light) Up My Life" by T. C. Fly

What butterfly is invincible?
Cocoon the Barbarian.

FLIP: I just bought a talking parrot for a
thousand dollars.
SKIP: What does it say?
FLIP: "You paid too much, you paid too much!"

What would you get if you crossed a canary and
a magician?
Cheep tricks.

LARRY: How come birds don't eat in restaurants?
BARRY: Because they like pecking their own
lunch.

What kind of birds always write in ink?
Pen-guins.

What's yellow and goes "rat-a-tat-tat"?
A chicken with a machine gun.

What would you get if you crossed a Slinky with
a young hen?
Spring chicken.

What goes "beep-beep-beep," "buck-buck-buck"?
A chicken at an automatic teller machine.

What would you get if you crossed a male turkey
with a bird of prey?
A tom-a-hawk.

When do skunks stuff turkeys?
  Stanksgiving.

When do snakes stuff turkeys?
  Fangsgiving.

What would you get if you crossed an owl with a babysitter?
  A whoo-te-nanny.

What would you get if you crossed a bat with a begonia?
  A plant that hangs upside down.

What do you get when you don't iron your moose?
  Bullwrinkle.

What do rabbits put on the back of their cars?
Thumper stickers.

Why did the rabbit go to the barber shop?
To get a hare-do.

How do rabbits go on long trips?
Via Trans-World Harelines.

What did the pet shop owner say when the boys fought over the rabbit?
"Stop pulling my hare!"

What do you get when you cross a toupee with a groundhog?
Six more wigs (weeks) of winter.

Who did the little girl horse fall in love with?
  The bay (boy) next door.

What did one mule say to the other?
  "I get a kick out of you."

What did the mule say to the sheep?
  "I get a kick out of ewe."

    Knock-knock!
      Who's there?
    Pasture.
      Pasture who?
    Pasture bedtime, isn't it?

What do you call the winner of a barnyard beauty contest?
  The Dairy Queen.

Why is it so tough to make cows laugh?
  Because they herd (heard) all the good ones.

What is the golden rule for cows?
  "Do unto udders . . ."

What would you get if you crossed a tramp with a cow?
  A bum steer.

JASON: I finally found the rattle in my car.

MASON: I'm glad to hear it.

JASON: I'm not—it was attached to a snake.

Snakes Alive!

What do country western snakes wear?
Venom (denim) jackets.

What do you take for snakebite?
Anti-hiss-tamines.

What do snakes do after a fight?
They hiss and make up.

What did the garden snake say to his wife?
"I wear the plants in the family."

What would you get if you crossed linguini with a boa constrictor?
Spaghetti that winds itself.

Where does the king of the boa constrictors stay when he's in Las Vegas?
Squeezer's (Caesar's) Palace.

What kind of snakes are useful in rainstorms?
  Windshield vipers.

Why did Mother Cobra put powder on her babies?
  To avoid viper (diaper) rash.

What kind of underwear do female snakes
wear?
  Co-bras.

Why did the snake swallow the flashlight?
  It wanted to shed some light.

What snakes like Raggedy Ann?
  Cottonmouths.

Why did the goat go to McDonald's?
To get a Kid's Meal.

What do goats eat for breakfast?
Goatmeal.

What do moths eat for breakfast?
Coatmeal.

What do termites eat for lunch?
Door jam (jamb) sandwiches.

Where do lambs buy their clothes?
Lamb shops.

What kind of suit would you wear to a kangaroo wedding?

A jump suit.

What do you call an Australian animal after it gets run over by a truck?

A duck-billed splattypus.

What could you give a kangaroo for his birthday that you couldn't give a frog?

A pocket watch.

Where do foster frogs come from?

Croaken homes.

What would you get if you crossed a frog with a pig?

A wart hog.

What do pigs enjoy most about casinos?

The slop (slot) machines.

Sign for "The King of the Jungle Moving Company"

WE DON'T TAKE YOUR MOVE LION DOWN "

What animal likes to go to museums?

The artvark (aardvark).

What's grey, dives in the swimming pool and goes "Ow!"?

An elephant with chlorine in his eyes.

Why did the elephant hang his trunk out the car window?

His turn signal was broken.

Why are elephants so smart?

Because they have a lot of grey matter.

How do you give an elephant a bath?

First you find a very large rubber duckie . . .

Why don't elephants like their kids to walk in line?

They believe children should be seen, not herded.

What do you call a camel that lives in a garbage pit?

Humpty Dumpty.

What did the boy do when his pet rodent used bad words?

He washed his mouse out with soap.

6. "SAY AHHHH... CHOO!"

SAY AAAH....

Why did the automobile cough?
It was car sick.

Where do sick fire trucks go?
To the hose-pital.

Where do sick boats go?
To the dock-tor.

What kind of doctors make fish look younger?
Plastic sturgeons.

MOM: Did you take an aspirin for that cold?
SON: Yes, I did.
MOM: Bayer?
SON: That's how I caught it in the first place.

How do you tell the difference between a Xerox machine and the flu?

One makes facsimiles and the other makes sick families.

What do you get when you cross James Bond with a pharmacist?

License to pill.

What's the best medicine for a sick hog?

Pig pen-acillin.

A duck with a Band-Aid on his nose went to see his doctor.

"Are you here about your beak?" asked the nurse.

"No," said the duck, "I'm here about my bill."

Why did the tree surgeon buy another office?
He was branching out.

Mr. Cummings went to see his doctor. The physician couldn't believe his eyes when he saw radishes growing out of Mr. Cummings' mouth.

"Well, that's unusual," said the doctor.

"You're not kidding!" replied Mr. Cummings. "I swallowed pumpkin seeds."

HEALTH TEACHER: How do we prevent tics?
HAROLD: Don't wear watches.

FIRST AID TEACHER: What happens if you're bitten by a rattlesnake?
CLASS JOKER: You're hiss-tory.

TEACHER: Why are you wearing a white sling on your arm?
SANDRA: You said I could wear anysling I want.

What did the pint of cream say to the quart of milk?
"My curdle (girdle) is killing me!"

"Doctor, Doctor, I Think I'm a . . ."

PATIENT: Doctor, doctor, I think I'm a radio!

DOCTOR: I'm sorry, you're not coming in too clearly.

PATIENT: Doctor, doctor, I think I'm a porcupine!

DOCTOR: Stop needling me!

PATIENT: Doctor, doctor, I think I'm a light bulb!

DOCTOR: Watt do you mean by that?

PATIENT: Doctor, doctor, I think I'm a cow!

DOCTOR: Just open your mouth and say "moo."

PATIENT: Thanks to your help, I no longer think I'm a kitty cat. How can I ever repay you?

DOCTOR: Well, for starters, you can take that ball of string out of your mouth.

When should you take your computer to the doctor?
When it loses its memory.

What did the book say to the therapist?
"I'm trying to find my shelf (myself)."

Why did the turtle see a psychiatrist?
He wanted to come out of his shell.

EYE PATIENT: I stepped on my glasses and broke them. Will the doctor have to examine me all over again?
NURSE: No, just your eyes.

What's a good remedy for squeaky infants?
Baby oil.

Why did one witch doctor eat the other witch doctor?

Because it's a doc-eat-doc (dog-eat-dog) world.

What do good doctors and obedient dogs have in common?

They both know how to heal (heel).

Who comes down the hospital chimney once a year and fills the stockings with bandages?

Santa Gauze.

What nursery rhyme camel had swollen glands?

Humpty Mumpty.

Why wasn't Eve afraid of getting the measles?

Because she already Adam.

What's big and scary and fills cavities?
  Dentist the Menace.

What did the dentist say to the computer?
  "This won't hurt a byte."

What do dentists like most about amusement parks?
  Molar coasters.

What would you get if you crossed novocaine with a skeleton?
  A numbskull.

MOTHER: Has your bad tooth stopped aching?
BOBBY: I don't know. The dentist kept it.

How are bad teeth like Thanksgiving turkeys?
  They both need a lot of filling.

Why was the little kid afraid to go to the dentist?
  He was gum shy.

What did the bad tooth say to the departing dentist?
  "Fill me in when you get back."

7. CLASSROOM CAPERS

What happened to the cannibal who ate his teacher?

He had to cook with substitutes.

What kind of exams do cannibals like?

Taste tests.

SCIENCE TEACHER: Can cats see better at night?

CLASS CLOWN: Yes, but they have trouble holding the flashlight.

Why was Silly Sarah kicked out of art school?

She drew a blank.

Why was the elephant expelled from school?
Because he trunked (flunked) out.

How do cows know what's going on at school?
They read the bull-etin boards.

Where do young cows eat lunch at school?
The calf-eteria.

He's so dumb all he could pass in school was the salt and pepper.

Joey Smith got so good at forging signatures he began charging his friends to write absentee notes for them. One day the principal found out and called him into the office.

"Well, Joey," said the principal, "you'd better have a good excuse for me."

"I do," Joey replied. "But it'll cost you."

What would you get if you crossed hopscotch with hookey?
Someone who likes to skip school.

TEACHER: Use "cultivate" in a sentence.
JIMMY: One winter morning it was too cultivate (cold to wait) for the bus so I took the subway.

My school is so hygiene-conscious that on every street corner we have a flossing guard.

Where do you put a sick ballpoint pen?
In an ink-u-bator.

What do you call the period of time when nerds ruled the earth?
The Dork Ages.

TEACHER: Who started this fight?
BILLY: Donald threw a rock at me, so I threw one back.
TEACHER: Why didn't you come to me?
BILLY: Because your aim isn't as good as mine.

What music did they play outside the castle?
Moat-zart.

What do geniuses use to get clear?
Mental floss.

Bus Wishes

How do ghosts get to school?
On a ghoul bus.

How do slobs get to school?
On a drool bus.

How do Santa's elves get to school?
On a Yule bus.

How do clowns get to school?
On a fool bus.

How do lifeguards get to school?
On a pool bus.

How do bullies get to school?
On a cruel bus.

How do bees get to school?
On a school buzz.

How do athletes get to school?
They walk.

Hannibal Cannibal Cafeteria Menu
Neck Tarines
Elbow Macaroni
Head Cheese
Toe Fu (tofu)
Butter Fingers

TEACHER: Why did you copy Larry's test?
SEYMOUR: What gave me away?
TEACHER: His name on your paper.

STAN: My nickname is Scissors.
DAN: Because you're so sharp?
STAN: No, because I always cut class.

Why did the elephant have to stay after school?
Because he missed the bus.

Why did the snake have to stay after school?
Because he hissed the bus.

Why did the autumn leaves have to stay after school?
Because they missed the gust.

TEACHER: How can you do so many stupid things in one day?
ANDREW: I get up early.

No matter what happened in the classroom, Mrs. McGilicuddy was the kind of teacher who never got upset.

One day a 747 crash-landed in the classroom and she said, "Who threw that?"

What do you call assignments from a Chinese cooking class?

Home-wok.

Upon returning from a field trip to the zoo, the principal asked Miss Dickinson how she enjoyed the outing.

"Oh, it was horrible," said Miss Dickinson. "The snakes stuck their tongues out and the monkeys kept making faces."

"Well, you know what they say," replied the principal. "Boas will be boas, and gorillas will be gorillas."

What would you get if you crossed a bookmobile with a fire engine?

A book (hook) and ladder truck.

What would you get if you crossed a librarian with a race car driver?

A speed reader.

How do librarians talk?

They speak volumes.

What do librarians' kids play at parties?

Follow the reader.

Why did the teacher send the chicken to the principal's office?

Because it kept pecking on the other kids.

Kids in My School Are Really Lazy . . .

How lazy are they?

They're so lazy their favorite game is Hide and Sleep.

They're so lazy their school bus has bunk beds.

They're so lazy they dress up as pillows on Halloween.

They're so lazy their idea of exercise is watching TV without a remote.

What do you call a Macintosh that falls off a table?
Apple turnover.

What happened to the computer that stayed out in the cold too long?
It got frostbyte.

What do you get when you cross a food processor with a word processor?
A blender that eats your words.

8. TV OR NOT TV ... THAT IS THE QUESTION

JOE: What do you call a talk show hosted by a vegetable?

MOE: Okra Winfrey.

What movie tells about a cowboy hero abandoned by his parents?

   "Home Alone Ranger."

STAN: What movie tells about a computer abandoned by his parents?

DAN: "Ohm Alone."

What movie tells about a great and powerful magician of swampland?
"The Wizard of Ooze."

What leg-rubbing bug wears a coonskin cap?
Davy Cricket.

What show features cabbage-head lawyers on the West Coast?
"L.A. Slaw."

What do you call a TV junkie whose house gets hit by a tornado?
A mashed couch potato.

He's so brainwashed by TV his parents bought him a VCR with On-Screen Deprogramming.

What did the VCR say to the radio?
"You just don't get the picture, do you?"

What did the remote control say to the VCR?
"May I be forward with you?"

What do VCR tapes do on their day off?
They unwind.

What do Smurfs sing?
The blues.

What does the Road Runner do when it can't sleep?

It counts beep.

How do sharks improve their TV reception?
With a satellite fish.

What was Bruce Wayne before he was Batman?
Bat boy.

Who's squeaky clean and lives in a cave?
Bathman.

Where does Robin the Boy Wonder take his showers?

In the bat-room (bathroom).

Who wears a mask and swings from curtain rods?

The Draped Crusader.

What's faster than a speeding bullet and able to clean tall buildings with a single sponge?

Soaperman.

What would you get if you crossed Donatello with a farm animal?

A teenage Moo-tant Turtle.

What do you get when you cross a reverend with
a talking horse?
Minister Ed.

What would you get if you crossed a "Star Wars"
movie with tomato sauce?
Jabba the Pizza Hut.

What would you get if you crossed fuzzy-haired
creatures with cookie dough?
Troll House Cookies.

What was Scrooge's favorite insect?
The humbug.

What's a termite's favorite movie star?
Woody Allen.

MINDY: What animated movie tells about a beautiful girl who falls in love with an ugly answering machine?

CINDY: "Beauty and the Beep."

What would you get if you crossed Bambi with an Avon representative?

A deer-to-deer salesman.

When was Mickey Mouse's girlfriend born?

Minnie moons ago.

ANDY: What sci-fi flick tells about an eighteenth century composer who travels in a time machine?

RANDY: "Bach to the Future."

What would you get if you crossed a hairdresser with Arnold Schwarzenegger?
The Perminator.

Who wears a mask and spreads grass seed wherever he goes?
The Lawn Ranger.

What kind of adventure films do vegetables enjoy?
Squashbucklers.

What kind of review did the critics give the fairy tale movie?
Two Thumbelinas Up.

How do D.J. spiders entertain their listeners?
They spin records.

What would you get if you crossed the Three Stooges with a snail?
Larry, Curly and Slo.

Knock-knock!
　Who's there?
One door.
　One door who?
One door woman (Wonder Woman).

What did Wonder Woman say to Spider Man?
"Don't bug me."

9. SCARED SILLY

What is the first thing you say when you enter a haunted house?

"Who ghost there?"

What ghostly painting hangs in the Louvre?

Moana Lisa.

What do ghosts play on rainy days?

Moan-opoly.

What kind of sheets do ghosts wear at the North Pole?

Sheets of ice.

64

What do you call six vampires to go?
A Drac Pack.

What do you call a depressed vampire?
Dracu-low.

Was the vampire race close?
Yes, it was neck and neck.

What did Dracula's mother hang over his crib?
A blood mobile.

Why did the baby vampire sleep in its parents' bed?
It kept having bat dreams.

Junior Dracula waited all year for the vampire carnival. When his turn came to ride on the giant bat, it was closing time.

"Please!" he pleaded, "Why can't I ride?"

"Sorry," replied the operator. "You missed your turn at bat."

What did the vampire say to the doctor?
"Take me to your bleeder."

Who guards the bloodmobile after hours?
The bite watchman.

What's the difference between vampires and leeches?

About half a pint.

NAN: What do you get when you cross Dracula and a mummy?

FRAN: I don't know, but if it bites you the bandages come in handy.

CINDY: What would you get if you crossed the Abominable Snowman and Dracula?

MINDY: A cold-blooded killer.

What would you get if you crossed Dracula and a werewolf?

A blood-sucking fur ball.

How do you tell when a werewolf is a failure?
When he wears a body toupee.

What do you get when you cross a werewolf with laundry?

Wash and wearwolf.

What would you get if you crossed a werewolf with Cinderella's guardian?

A hairy godmother.

Who is wicked and wears glass slippers?
  Sin-derella.

What kind of witchcraft does a dentist practice?
  Plaque magic.

What is the witches' national anthem?
  "Deep in the Heart of Hexes."

How did the warlock take his bride on their
honeymoon?
  On his groomstick.

What's a ghoul's favorite ice cream?
  Cookies and scream.

What would you get if you crossed a ghoul with
a cow?
  A ghost beef sandwich.

What would you get if you crossed the walking dead with stinging insects?
  Zom-bees.

What do you call a zombie who works for the post office?
  A dead letter carrier.

What do zombie magicians say when they do a trick?
  "Abra-cadaver."

What would you get if you crossed a St. Bernard with a zombie?
  A dog that buries itself.

What do zombies put on their mashed potatoes?
  Grave-y.

Name That Creature

It's seven feet tall, wallows in mud, and has a huge snout.
Pig Foot.

It's tall, hairy, lives in the Himalayas and does three hundred situps a day.
The Abdominal Snowman.

It lives beneath the waters of a Scottish lake and always leaves its room dirty.
The Loch Mess Monster.

It's a white horse with a long pointed vegetable protruding from its forehead.
Unicorn on the Cob.

What would you get if you crossed a nuclear scientist with a creepy clan?
The Atoms Family.

BABY MONSTER: Can I have a mummy for Christmas?
MOTHER MONSTER: Yes, but you'll have to wrap it yourself.

What's big and terrible and trips a lot?
Clodzilla.

PHIL: Why did Godzilla wait till the end of the movie to eat the coin factory?

WILL: He thought it was an after-dinner mint.

Why did Godzilla swallow the freighter loaded with cocoa beans?
He loved chocolate ships (chips).

Why did the superstitious sea captain refuse a cargo of duck feathers?
He didn't want his ship to go down.

What did the crocodile say to Captain Hook?
"Give me a hand, will you?"

Why did Captain Hook go to the thrift shop?
He wanted to find a second-hand bargain.

BARRY: Why did King Kong wear a baseball glove to the airport?

LARRY: He had to catch a plane.

What would you get if you crossed a goose with a 60-foot ape?
Honk Kong.

70

How do you know when a monster's not at home?
His answering machine is turned on.

What would you get if you crossed a bike with a monster?
A vicious cycle.

What has one wheel and moves by itself?
The Invisible Man on a unicycle.

Why did the Invisible Man go crazy?
Out of sight, out of mind.

Why was the Invisible Man heartbroken?
Because his girlfriend told him she couldn't see him anymore.

What rock band do skeletons listen to?
The Rolling Bones.

What did the mad scientist say to Igor when he dropped the bottle of gray matter?
"You scatterbrain!"

What did the dragon say to the gallant knight?
"You slay me."

Why did the man look for buried treasure in the dragon's cave?
He was seeking flame and fortune.

JUNIOR CANNIBAL: What's for dinner?
MOTHER CANNIBAL: We're having company.

What do ghosts do around a campfire?
They tell scary people stories.

Why was the ghost happy at the wedding reception?
She caught the boo-quet.

A Ghostly Riddle

A ghostbuster went into a haunted house to take pictures of a poltergeist. Spotting the spirit posing at the top of the stairs, he clicked away until the entire roll was finished. Later, when he had the film developed, all the pictures were underexposed. What happened to the photographs?

The spirit was willing, but the flash was weak.

What would you get if you crossed a zombie with a clown?
Someone who dies laughing.

What would you get if you crossed a farmer with a zombie?
Someone who raises the dead.

Why did Dr. Jekyll cry when he fell?
He skinned his Hyde.

Who were the first monsters to fly?
The Fright Brothers.

CANNIBAL TEACHER: Why should hands be washed before eating?
CANNIBAL STUDENT: Who wants to eat dirty hands?

When the lease on his apartment ran out, Mr. Hardy called the "Poltergeist Moving Company." After waiting three days, however, no one showed up.

"When are you leaving?" asked his landlord anxiously.

"When the spirit moves me," replied Mr. Hardy.

What do ghosts like best about computers?
Spreadsheets.

What did the mummy movie director say after shooting the last take?
"That's a wrap!"

10. QUICHE AND MAKEUP

What's the best way to mail a pizza?
With food stamps.

What's a cannibal's favorite snack?
Fri-toes.

Why did Silly Sally attach a rocket to her hamburger?
She liked really fast food.

Knock-knock!
  Who's there?
Liver
  Liver who?
Liver 'round here?

Knock-knock!
  Who's there?
Quiche.
  Quiche who?
Quiche me, you fool!

What's the difference between tuna fish and a piano tuner?

A piano tuner doesn't go well on toast.

Why did the bean help the old woman across the street?

He was hoping to join the Boy Sprouts.

Sourpuss Phil fell off his boat and was immediately devoured by a shark.

"Tasty?" asked another shark.

"No," replied the first, "it was a bitter Phil to swallow."

What do mice use to make sandwiches?
Shortbread.

If you eat lady fingers with your hands what do you eat with your feet—*tofu?*

MOM: How about a dip with your crackers?
TOM: No, thanks, I don't want to get crumbs in the pool.

BILL: What did the teaspoon say to the measuring cup?
JILL: "May I level with you?"

What did the chef say to the hungry watch?
"How about seconds?"

Knock-knock!
  Who's there?
Waiter.
  Waiter who?
Waiter (wait till) your father gets home!

Knock-knock!
  Who's there?
Lemon Meringue.
  Lemon Meringue who?
Lemon Meringue the bell, but nobody answered.

What would you get if you crossed Noah's ark with a vegetable?
Zoo-chini.

What's orange and jumps out of airplanes?
Carrot-troopers.

On a hot day a thirsty man rushed into a restaurant, drank the largest glass of water he could find, and then sat down at a table.

"Would you like to see a menu?" asked the waitress.

"I'd like another glass of water like the one you had out front," replied the still thirsty man.

"Hey, Harry!" the waitress shouted. "I found the idiot who drank our aquarium!"

What do gamblers eat for dessert?
Dice pudding.

What dessert can you eat in the ocean?
Sponge cake.

What savage warrior ate his way through most of central Europe?
Attila the Ton.

What did the cavemen eat for lunch?
Club sandwiches.

What did snobby Neanderthals eat?
Cave-iar.

What did medieval cannibals eat for dinner?
Peasant Under Glass.

Where does pasta go to lose weight?
Spa-ghettis.

What cartoon animal weighs the least?
Skinny-the-Pooh.

What do you get when you spill vinegar on the curtains?
Sour drapes (grapes).

What would you get if you crossed stinking yellow slime with good-for-nothing green slime?
Stinking good-for-nothing yellow-green slime.

What did one bath toy say to the other bath toy?
"You rubber duckie me the wrong way!"

What did the pancake say to the syrup?
"Stick with me—you'll go places."

11. CRIME TIME

How do you grill hamburgers?
First, you read them their rights . . .

How are hamburgers sent to jail?
In a patty wagon.

What did the oyster say to the gem?
"What's a nice pearl like you doing in a place like this?"

Where do cabbages go after they're arrested?
To a court of slaw.

Where do they put thieving tomatoes?
Behind salad bars.

TRAFFIC COP: Why didn't you stop when I blew my whistle?

DRIVER: I'm a little deaf.

TRAFFIC COP: Don't worry, you'll get your hearing tomorrow.

OFFICER: You can't park there!

DRIVER: Why not? The sign says "Fine for Parking."

POLICEMAN: Your driver's license says you should be wearing glasses.

MOTORIST: I have contacts.

POLICEMAN: I don't care how much pull you've got, you're still getting a ticket.

The World's Silliest
Musician Joke

A down-and-out musician was playing his guitar on a street corner. Striding over, an angry policeman asked: "May I see your permit?"

"I don't have one," said the musician.

"In that case, you'll have to accompany me," said the cop.

"Cool," exclaimed the musician. "What do you want to sing?"

What did the thumbtack say to the bulletin board?

"This is a stickup!"

POLICE EXAMINER: If you were by yourself in a police car and were pursued by a gang of criminals in another car doing 60 miles an hour, what would you do?

POLICE CANDIDATE: Seventy.

What do you call a psychopath who scrapes green, fuzzy stuff off trees?

A moss murderer.

JUDGE: Why did you steal the ballpoint?

CROOK: I haven't got an inkling.

JUDGE: One year in the pen.

JUDGE: Haven't I seen you somewhere before?

CROOK: I gave your daughter singing lessons.

JUDGE: Thirty years!

LAWYER: I've got good news and bad news.

PRISONER: What's the bad news?

LAWYER: They're still going to electrocute you at sunrise.

PRISONER: What's the good news?

LAWYER: I got the voltage reduced.

Why was the ghost found innocent?
Because he had an ali-boo.

What game do farm kids play in the cornfields?
Cobs and robbers.

What happened to the cookie on the witness stand?
He crumbled under oath.

What's squiggly, sharp and very dangerous?
A worm with an icepick.

Why was the bird arrested?
For blue jay walking.

SKIP: What's an owl's favorite mystery?
FLIP: A whoooo-dunit.

What detective is also a barber?
Sherlock Combs.

What Oriental chef is also a detective?
Sherwok Holmes.

What do English teachers and judges have in common?
They both like long sentences.

Why was the dishwasher arrested?
For panhandling.

What would you get if you crossed a dill with a thief?
A pickle-pocket.

What kind of shoes do secret agents wear?
Hush Puppies.

Why are poisonous trees more dangerous than guard dogs?
Their bark is worse than their bite.

What did the dealer say to the deck of cards?
"I can't deal with you anymore."

12. HAPPILY EVER LAUGHTER!

What did Chicken Little say when the pig pen fell over?

"The sty is falling, the sty is falling!"

What do you call a fairy tale about a white frog who lives with a bunch of dwarfs?

Snow Wart.

What did Snow White like to read to the dwarfs at night?

Short stories.

Why did the limo driver leave his job after five years?

He had nothing to chauffeur (show for) it.

Why did the shy conductor stand with his back to the orchestra?

He couldn't face the music.

What did the accountant do in the circus?

He juggled the books.

WILL: Why are you grounded?
BILL: I tried to fill my father's shoes.
WILL: Did you succeed?
BILL: Yes, I filled them with tacks.

MOE: My uncle's a farmer and a pool player.
JOE: I guess he has to mind his peas and cues.

What do baby ships like after a nighttime story?
Someone to tug them into bed.

What fairy tale tells about a wooden puppet who wears cloth diapers?
Safety Pin-occhio.

What's a pig's favorite fairy tale?
Hamsel and Gruntel.

What has four wheels and diaper rash?
A baby in a shopping cart.

What's the difference between prospectors and butchers?
Prospectors stake their claims, butchers claim their steaks.

What's the difference between the Coast Guard and an old wreck?
The Coast Guard goes to sea, an old wreck ceases to go.

What's the difference between a Boy Scout and an answering machine repairman?
A Boy Scout's motto is: "Be Prepared." An answering machine repairman's motto is: "Beep Repaired."

JOE: My mother got fired from the telephone
   company.
MOE: What happened—did she miss her calling?

What kind of cars do rubber bands drive?
   Stretch limos.

What did the little tire want to be when he
grew up?
   A big wheel.

Why was the automobile mechanic fired?
   He took too many brakes (breaks).

How is a tailor like a lawyer?
   They both press your suit.

RANDY: I read this study that said every time
   you breathe, a person dies.
SANDY: I didn't think my breath was that bad!

CLARA: I read this pamphlet that said "By the
   time you finish reading this paragraph,
   someone will have died."
SARA: What did you do?
CLARA: I stopped reading right away.

What do you give a snowman for his birthday?
   A cake of ice.

What's the difference between a target shooter and a dry cleaning person?

One spots the mark, the other marks the spot.

What's the difference between an object used to ride the waves and an unemployed peasant?

One's a surf board, the other's a bored serf.

What's the difference between a cattle herder and a locomotive driver?

One trains the steers, the other steers the trains.

What's the difference between a boat builder and a mail order mannequin company?

One shapes ships, the other ships shapes.

What would you get if you crossed a silent performer with a psychic?

Mime over matter.

What would you get if you crossed a psychic with a store closing?

A Going-Out-of-My-Mind Sale.

What do you call a mime in shining armor?

Silent Knight.

What did one torpedo say to the other torpedo?

"Are you sinking what I'm sinking?"

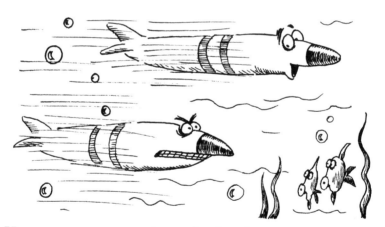

How can you recognize a hothead?

By his sideburns.

What would you get if you crossed a hillbilly with Santa Claus?

A ho-ho-ho down.

A Chip Off the Old Block

What do architects' kids play with?
City blocks.

What do butchers' kids play with?
Chopping blocks.

What do construction workers' kids play with?
Building blocks.

What do novelists' kids play with?
Writers' blocks.

What do psychics' kids play with?
Mental blocks.

What do prison wardens' kids play with?
Cell blocks.

What kind of fight breaks out in a shopping center?
A free-for-mall.

What kind of dance lessons are offered at shopping malls?
Mallroom dancing.

What has a nice trunk, but never goes on a trip?
A tree.

Why don't trees go on trips?
Because they're afraid to leaf home.

What kind of tree keeps you warm?
A fur (fir) tree.

What would you get if you crossed a pig with
a tree?
A pork-u-pine.

What would you get if you crossed a
sledgehammer with a Valentine?
A real heartbreaker.

What would you get if you crossed a king's wife
with a car rental agency?
The Queen of Hertz.

What did the lumberjack say to the tree stump?
"Hollow down there!"

What did the preacher say at the robot's funeral?
"Rust in peace."

About the Authors

About the Authors

Philip Yates is a stand-up comic and playwright and a member of the Philadelphia-based Laugh-A-Roni Players. He has performed in comedy clubs in Delaware, Pennsylvania and New Jersey. He received his B.A. from Widener University and his master's in theater from Villanova University, where his play *Rapid Eye Movements* was performed recently. He lives in Prospect Park, Pennsylvania.

Matt Rissinger is also a member of Laugh-A-Roni. He, like Phil, has his roots in stand-up comedy. He and his wife, Maggie, live near Valley Forge, Pennsylvania. Matt uses his daughters, Rebecca and Emily, to kid-test his jokes. If they don't find them funny, Matt is sent to bed without his supper. Matt holds a master's degree from Temple University's School of Communications.

INDEX